On the Run

by

Stephanie Baudet

Illustrated by Kris Evans

First Published
October 2009 in Great Britain by

PUBLISHING

A CIP record for this work is available from the British Library

ISBN-10: 1-905637-83-7
ISBN-13: 978-1-905637-83-6

Typeset by Educational Printing Services Limited

Educational Printing Services Limited

E-mail: enquiries@eprint.co.uk Website: www.eprint.co.uk

Contents

Joyriders

People began screaming.

Tina's eyes snapped open and she sat up. The sand was hot under her fingers. She shaded her eyes so she could see what was happening. Her sister Lesley had been sunbathing on the beach too.

'What is it?' asked Lesley.

A small boat had gone mad. It was zigzagging backwards and forwards close to the shore. People were trying to run out of the sea. Parents were snatching their young children out of the water.

The boat spun round spraying an arc of water into the air. Then it raced out to sea and round the rocky headland.

Tina stood up. What maniacs! It must be those joyriders they'd heard about on TV. They stole boats instead of cars. They could have killed someone. Her heart was thudding.

A police siren wailed.

'They're crazy!' Lesley said. 'Are you sure that boy you met last night isn't one of them?'

'Why should he be?' Tina snapped. She knew her sister was jealous.

Lesley grinned. 'Well. He said his parents owned a big yacht. I think it's a lie.'

Tina felt anger surge up inside her and she gritted her teeth to stop the cross words coming out. She didn't want to have a row with Lesley too. Not after the row with Mum and Dad last night. She needed a friend.

'Let's go back to the cottage,' she said.

They walked back along the edge of the sea. The foam tickled their toes.

'There's Peter!' said Tina. 'He's sitting on the same rock as last night. You see, he can't be one of the joyriders.'

She called to him and he looked up and squinted into the sun. It was difficult to tell if he was glad to see them or not. He looked pleased but wary.

'This is my sister Lesley.'

Peter smiled. Then he hurled a pebble into the sea.

'That's not the way to do it,' said Tina.

'Do what?'

'Ducks and drakes.' She picked up a pebble and threw it. It bounced a couple of times before sinking. 'It's too rough,' she said. 'It needs to be dead calm. My record is five bounces.'

'Did you see the joyriders?' asked Lesley.

'Joyriders, in the sea?'

'Yes. In a boat. Didn't you see it on TV?'

Peter shook his head.

'I went to see *your* boat,' said Tina.

His head jerked up. 'My boat?'

'Sorry, your yacht. The *Erica Banner*. You said it was moored here. No-one was onboard.'

'Oh, that's not ours. Mum and Dad must have gone fishing,' said Peter. He was looking at the ground and not looking into her eyes. He's embarrassed, thought Tina. Being rich must make you feel bad sometimes.

'What's yours called then?' asked Lesley. Tina wished her sister would keep out of it.

'The . . . um . . . *The Mermaid,*' he said, looking up and smiling. 'I'd forgotten because she's new.'

'Time to go home for lunch,' said Lesley.

Tina bent down and put on her flip-flops. 'Well?' she said as soon as they were far enough away. She couldn't help feeling smug.

'He's good looking,' said Lesley, 'but I don't trust him. I can tell when someone is lying.'

Tina gave her a playful push. Her sister was so pathetic. She was wrong if she thought she could ruin her holiday. Tina was going to have a good time in spite of her sister and her parents.

The Funfair

The next day, Tina was walking on the beach, deep in her thoughts.

'Hi,' said a voice.

Tina looked round and grinned. It was Peter.

'So, all alone today? Where's Lesley?'

Tina shrugged. 'She went into town. I just didn't fancy going with her. Where is your yacht? I was hoping to see it.'

She watched his face. He was embarrassed again.

'Why don't we go to the funfair?' she said.

Peter turned and smiled at her. Then he delved into his pockets and frowned. 'I didn't bring any money,' he said.

'I'll lend you some,' said Tina.

'If you're sure . . .'

''Course. Come on, let's walk to town along the beach.'

A gust of wind from the sea ruffled his hair. He looked so cool standing there. Tina was so happy she wanted to laugh out loud for no apparent reason. She took off her flip-flops and they both ran. She felt the warm sand ooze between her toes. This was the best she had felt for a long time.

'Isn't that your sister?' said Peter as they reached the town.

Tina's happiness dissolved in a blink. Just now she didn't want her sister butting in.

Lesley had seen them and ran over. 'There's a talent competition this afternoon,' she said. 'I'm going to enter. Stuart Cresswell is judging the finals.' Then she was off again.

'What is she going to do?' asked Peter.

'She'll sing.'

'Who is Stuart Cresswell?'

Tina couldn't believe there was anyone on the planet who didn't know.

'Where have you been? He's just about the coolest singer around. Leslie has posters of him all over her bedroom walls. He has a Siamese cat which he takes everywhere, isn't that nice?'

'You like cats, then?' said Peter. 'I do too.'

Tina turned and smiled at him, delighted. They seemed to have so much in common.

The funfair was crowded but Tina loved the hustle and bustle. For a while she felt as if she was five years old instead of nearly fourteen.

* * *

After a great time at the fair, they headed back along the beach.

'Now what about your yacht?' Tina asked. 'Will your parents be back yet?'

Peter just shrugged. Tina felt a wave of anger. Why was he being like this? She'd had a fun afternoon and he was spoiling it.

'Tomorrow then,' she said, 'I'll come to the marina around eight!'

'OK then,' Peter agreed reluctantly.

'Then what shall we do? I can't afford the funfair again.'

'I haven't forgotten what I owe you,' said Peter. 'I'll pay you back.'

'Pay back what?' said a voice behind them. It was Lesley.

Peter turned. 'How did you get on with the competition?'

'Pay back what?' said Lesley again.

'We went to the funfair. Peter hadn't brought any money and I lent him some,' replied Tina. Just what was her sister's problem?

'Right,' said Lesley, sarcastically.

Peter said goodbye and sloped off back towards the town.

Tina swung round to face her sister. 'Why are you so nasty to him?'

'I don't trust him.'

'You're just jealous!'

'Jealous!' Lesley grabbed Tina's arm. 'Tina, I don't trust him. I'm afraid for you. All this talk about a yacht and it's never there. He wears the same clothes every day. Doesn't that seem odd to you?'

'I'm going to see the yacht early tomorrow.'

Lesley laughed. 'Yeah, right. And what about the money? You won't see that again.'

Tina gritted her teeth. Sometimes she really hated her sister. She strode on ahead and they didn't speak again all the way back to the cottage.

The Boat Trip

'Are you coming?' asked Tina the next morning, as she pulled on her denim shorts and tried to fasten the zip.

Lesley laughed. 'You won't be able to sit down in them.'

Tina grinned too. 'I don't care. I'm not a diet freak. This is just how I am. So, are you coming?'

Lesley nodded.

They had almost reached the marina when a small boat roared round the headland. Then the motor cut out and it drifted in to the beach.

Tina shaded her eyes. 'It's Peter!'

Peter waved and they ran to him.

'Get in,' he said. 'I'll take you for a ride.'

'But what about the yacht?' said Tina. 'I really wanted to see it.'

Peter just smiled and Tina felt a spark of anger and doubt. 'Don't tell me. They've gone out already.' Perhaps Lesley was right. She looked at her sister; she had an odd look on her face and was staring at Peter and frowning.

'Are you coming too?' Peter asked Lesley.

'She's afraid of water,' said Tina.

'Thanks,' said Lesley, 'just tell everyone my secrets.'

Peter didn't laugh. 'It's very calm,' he said.

Lesley had a scared look in her eyes. 'You should ask Mum and Dad.'

Tina laughed. 'You don't have to come. Why should I ask Mum and Dad? I'm not afraid of water.'

'Please, Tina. Don't go. It might be dangerous!'

Tina ignored her. 'She's not coming. Let's go.'

'Yes, I am,' sighed Lesley.

The two girls got into the boat. As Peter turned to start the outboard motor, Lesley whispered, 'It's him! He is one of the joyriders. It was his face on TV.'

Tina wished her sister had not come. She moved away from her to sit near Peter at the back of the boat. He had the motor running and they sped away from the shore.

After a while, Tina leant forward to see how Lesley was coping. Her sister's face was pale and she clung to the side of the boat and stared into the distance. Well it was her own fault. She didn't have to come.

The boat slowed. 'If you're really scared, Lesley,' said Peter, 'I'll take you back.' He started to turn the boat.

When they reached the beach Tina watched her sister stagger ashore.

'Aren't you coming, Tina?'

'Of course not. I'll see you later.'

Now there was just her and Peter. Tina sighed and settled back in the boat. She lifted her face to the wind and let it blow through her hair.

'You are lucky, Peter. Is this the yacht's dinghy? If the yacht sinks your parents won't have a life-boat.'

'Shut up about the yacht!'

Tina sat up. 'I thought you would be proud to show it to me. Don't you want me to meet your parents?'

Peter swung the boat towards the open sea and raced along. Tina clung to the side.

'Peter! Slow down!'

He took no notice. The boat flew along, hitting the tops of the waves with big thumps.

'Peter!'

He had gone mad. She tried to grab the lever to slow the boat down but he pushed her hard and she fell back into the boat.

Then, with a splutter, the motor died.

There was silence. Only the slap of the waves against the side.

'Why have we stopped?' asked Tina sharply.

Peter pulled the starter cord but nothing happened.

'I didn't stop it.'

'What's the matter then?'

'How should I know?' said Peter, slumping in his seat.

'But I thought you knew about boats? Is there petrol in it? Your dad wouldn't leave it empty, would he?'

'It isn't my dad's boat.'

Tina stared at him. 'Whose is it then?'

Peter shrugged. 'I nicked it.'

So Lesley was right . . .

'You stole a boat?!' She looked around panicking. There was nothing but open sea. For the first time she began to feel afraid.

Peter put his head in his hands and started to cry. Tina had never seen a boy his age cry. She said nothing. The boat rocked gently and a seagull screeched overhead.

She let him cry.

At last he said, 'I lied about everything. There is no yacht. I've run away from home.'

'Where are you staying?'

'In an old beach hut.'

'Don't you get on with your parents either?'

'They have split up. I live with my mum, but she has a new boyfriend and they don't want me. I've come to find my dad. He lives here in Greenbay.'

'Haven't you been to see him yet?' asked Tina.

'How do I know he wants me?' said Peter. 'He never asked me to come.'

He was afraid to find out. Tina reached out and put her hand on his. 'I'll come with you,' she said.

He squeezed her hand and it felt nice but a cool wind made her shiver. She took her hand away. Was he telling the truth now or still lying? Once someone had lied you could never really trust them.

Tina looked around. 'Which way to shore?' She watched his face as he squinted all round.

'You don't know, do you?'

He hesitated and then shook his head. Peter's days of pretending were over.

Cornwall Gardens

Tina sat huddled in the boat. The wind was cold and it wasn't fun any more.

Peter was quiet. He sat with his hand on the tiller, staring into the distance. He'd managed to get the boat started again and now they could see the shore.

'I'm frozen,' said Tina, 'and I'm hungry. Mum will go mad. It's after one o'clock.'

Peter looked at her and his eyes were soft. 'Just say you are sorry. We got lost.'

'I can't tell them about the boat. It's stolen. That's the trouble with lies. They get bigger and bigger.'

They landed on the other side of the marina.

'I'll leave the boat here,' said Peter. He looked around but no-one was watching.

'Let's go and see your dad this afternoon,' Tina said. 'Can't you live with who you want?'

Peter shook his head. 'Mum has custody until I'm sixteen. That's not until next year and I can't wait that long. I've had enough. She doesn't want me anyway.'

Tina took his arm. 'Come and have lunch with us!'

Peter laughed, 'You are only inviting me so you won't get told off.'

It was the first time she had heard him laugh. They ran all the way back to the cottage.

Tina's mum was cross but she was nice to Peter. Lesley was very quiet and looked pale but she was nice to Peter too. What a strange lot her family were, thought Tina. Only her father was his normal self and chatted away to Peter.

Later it turned much cooler and looked like rain. Many people were in the cafés and amusement arcades.

'Where does your dad live?' asked Tina.

'Cornwall Gardens.'

'Do you know where that is?'

Peter nodded. 'I've been there.'

Tina kept quiet. This was difficult for Peter and he would not want her chattering. How awful not to know whether he would be welcome or not. She was glad her parents were still together. She looked at his face. It was blank, like a mask, hiding his feelings.

Cornwall Gardens was on a steep hill. From the top you could probably see the sea but Tina did not turn round to look. Peter had stopped.

'It's this one,' he said.

It was a neat brick house with a bay window. There were flowers in a window box and a tiny front garden.

Peter stared at the house. Then he grasped her hand and she realised how much she liked him. But he needed her strength now, not her love.

He let go of her hand and walked up to the front door and rang the bell.

Tina felt her heart thumping as they waited. Then the door opened and a woman stood there. She was dressed in jeans and a red top.

'Yes?'

The colour drained from Peter's face. He turned and ran back through the gate and down the hill. Tina said sorry to the woman and then ran after him. She guessed why he had run away. He thought the woman must be his dad's new girlfriend . . .

Lesley is Threatened

Peter wasn't in any of the beach huts. Tina walked along the sand looking into each of them. Where could he have gone?

At last she went back to her cottage. It was beginning to rain. Her parents were watching a film so she just waved and went to the room she shared with her sister.

Lesley was lying on her bed.

'You've got to help me find Peter,' said Tina. 'I've looked in all the beach huts.'

Lesley sat up and frowned. 'What do you mean? You were with him, and why would he be in a beach hut when he has a yacht?'

Tina shook her head. 'There is no yacht.'

Lesley grinned. 'I knew he was lying! He never looked you in the eye.'

'Don't look so smug! He's run away from home.' Tina felt angry. She'd been made to look a fool believing Peter's lies and why should she have expected Lesley to understand? She turned and left the bedroom, unsure where she was going to go.

'No, wait!' Lesley sprang off the bed and ran after her. 'It might help if you told me the whole story.'

Tina took a deep breath and turned towards her sister. 'His parents have split up. He says his mum has a new partner and doesn't want him. His dad lives here. We went to see him but there was just a woman there. I'm sure Peter thinks his dad won't want him either if he has a new girlfriend.'

'He might.'

'I know, but try telling Peter that. He's really upset. He ran away and I don't know where to look.' But she did! There *was* a place he could go if he wanted to be alone. 'Our cave!' said Tina. 'Maybe he knows about that. Let's go and look.'

'No!' Lesley had gone pale.

'Why not? We often go there. He's probably found it too!' Tina rushed out of the cottage, Lesley following her.

Short of breath, Lesley tried to speak, grabbing her sister's arm. Tina shook her off and carried on running across the dunes to the beach, with Lesley still behind her. She didn't stop running until she reached the cave. Then she stopped and stared.

'Look at this!' she spat out. 'Pigs! This can't be Peter's stuff. It stinks. He may be homeless but he's clean.' She looked round at the dirty sleeping bags.

Lesley was standing outside the cave looking around nervously. 'Come on, Tina. It's not our cave any more. They've contaminated it. It's the boat thieves, the joyriders. I came here earlier today, that's what I was trying to tell you!'

Tina stared at her sister. 'You saw them?'

Lesley nodded. 'And they saw me.'

She was almost in tears as she turned away and Tina rushed after her. 'What happened?'

'I overheard their plans. They're going to steal the *Erica Banner*. I tried to get away but I slipped and they heard me.' She began to shake and Tina grabbed her hand.

'What? What did they do? We've got to tell Mum and Dad.'

'No! They threatened me. They were horrible! There were two of them, Dave and . . . and Bernie. They grabbed me. It was awful, Tina. We've got to get away from here before they come back.'

The sisters ran back across the dunes and Tina went back to the huts, just in case Peter had gone there.

Exhausted, she finally arrived back at the cottage just as her family was getting ready to go out for their evening meal.

Terror on the Big Wheel

Tina's eyes felt sore from lack of sleep. She had been awake half the night worrying about Peter. She must get up and go and look for him again. Where was he? Had he run away again? She remembered how he had looked as he'd run from his dad's house.

The door opened and Lesley looked in. She was still pale and didn't smile. Tina felt cross. She had enough worries with Peter. She didn't need Lesley's problems too. Those youths were all hot air. They wouldn't do anything if Lesley kept her mouth shut.

'I'll help you look for Peter,' said Lesley. 'Mum and Dad are going out somewhere and my semi-finals for the competition aren't until this afternoon.'

Ten minutes later they were walking along the beach towards the town. Lesley seemed nervous and kept looking around.

'What's the matter with you?'

'Don't shout,' said Lesley.

'I'll shout if I want to. What . . .'

Lesley grabbed her arm and pulled her down behind a dune. 'Sshh!'

As Tina wrenched her arm free and tried to struggle to her feet she heard voices. Two youths were coming along the beach towards them. Then she knew. These boys had ruined their cave with their stinking sleeping bags. She'd tell them!

Lesley gripped her arm harder as if she could read her mind.

'It's tonight,' said one of the boys. 'He's judging that stupid talent competition. We've just got a couple of hours.' He clicked his fingers in the air. 'Then we'll be rich!' Their laughter faded as they walked away.

Lesley's grip tightened. 'I know whose boat it is! It must belong to Stuart Cresswell.'

'But why steal it?' asked Tina. 'Everyone will recognise it.'

Lesley shrugged.

'This is silly,' said Tina. 'We have to find Peter. That's more important than a stupid yacht.'

They looked everywhere again. In the beach huts, at the marina and under the pier. They looked among the crowd on the beach and in the town, but he was not there.

They didn't find a body washed up on the shore either, thought Tina. This afternoon she would go and see his dad. Maybe Peter had gone back later and met him.

* * * *

Tina stood outside forty-two Cornwall Gardens. She felt silly. What could she say to Peter's dad?

She marched up to the front door. Her mouth was dry. She rang the bell and listened for footsteps. There were none.

As she turned to leave, the door to the next house opened. The lady who stood there was the same lady they had seen the previous day. Tina wondered if she had come to the right house.

'Can I help you, dear? Mr Penrose isn't in.'

'I'm a friend of his son, Peter.'

'He's at work.' The woman looked at her watch. 'He'll be home soon. Can I give him a message?'

Tina decided to be direct. 'Is that your house? I just wondered why . . .'

'Why I was over there yesterday when you came? I do his housework. He's a busy man. Was that Peter who was with you yesterday? Mr Penrose talks about him a lot but he didn't say he was coming to visit.'

'It's a surprise,' said Tina. 'But . . . he's upset about something and I can't find him.'

It must have sounded a weird story as the woman looked puzzled. 'I'll tell Mr Penrose you were here,' she said.

So the woman was only a neighbour and not a girlfriend. If only she could find Peter and tell him.

As she passed the funfair she heard her name called. It was Lesley.

'I'm in the finals!' she said. 'Ten of us have to perform in front of Stuart Cresswell!' Her eyes were dancing and she looked much happier.

Then Tina felt someone grasp her shoulder hard. She spun round and saw two youths facing her. It was the two they had seen on the beach. The one with his hand on her shoulder laughed and she could smell the beer on his breath.

'We thought you girls would like a ride on the Big Wheel,' he said. As he spoke he pushed her forward. 'Girls like going on a good scary ride don't they, Bernie? They love to scream.'

'Yep, they do Dave!'

There were people all around and Tina tried to shout but no sound came from her mouth. It was normal for funfairs to be noisy with shouts and screams.

The boys pushed them onto a seat. When the wheel began to move, Dave let go of Tina's arm.

The seat had nearly reached the highest point on the wheel.

'How do you like it so far?' said Dave.

Neither of the girls spoke. Dave nudged Tina. 'Hey! I'm speaking to you! Lost your tongue?'

Bernie laughed. 'A pity they can't lose their tongues for good. Then we wouldn't have to worry.'

'You haven't answered,' said Dave. He sounded angry now. 'Don't you like Big Wheels?'

'Usually,' said Tina.

'So you don't like our company then?'

What were they planning to do? Tina looked over the edge. It was a long way down.

The wheel stopped as they reached the top and they swung backwards and forwards. There was nothing in front of them and the roofs of the town were far below. It was as if they were alone up there.

The seat was swinging faster and higher.

'Please stop,' said Lesley. 'We won't say anything.' Her voice was shaky. Tina looked at her and their eyes met. They both knew that the youths were swinging the chair on purpose. Soon the only thing keeping them from falling was the safety bar. It was not a strong bar. You were not meant to swing the seats.

'What were you doing snooping in the cave?' growled Dave.

'It . . . it's our cave. We like to go there.'

'And you are not going to tell anyone what you heard?'

Both girls shook their heads.

'But you did tell your sister,' said Bernie to Lesley. 'Shows you can't trust girls to keep their mouths shut, don't it?'

'I think they will,' said Dave. The seat was swinging less now and Tina took a deep sigh of relief as the wheel began to move again. 'Another ride up here might not be so much fun.'

Tina had never been so pleased to feel the ground beneath her feet. She felt very shaky. And this nightmare wasn't over yet.

She still had to find Peter.

And Lesley had to sing in the competition.

And while that was going on, the youths would be stealing the yacht.

Telling Secrets

They almost missed Peter.

They were so shaken by the threatening ride on the Big Wheel that all they wanted to do was go back to the cottage.

They were hurrying along the main street in silence. As they passed a café, someone tapped on the window. Peter was sitting at a table with a man. Both were smiling.

Tina was relieved to see him. The two girls went into the café.

'Peter! We've been looking for you.' Tina looked from him to the man.

'This is my dad,' said Peter. 'After you spoke to Mrs Butts he came looking for me. I was at the station waiting for a train to go back to Mum's.'

Peter's dad smiled. 'Thank you for trying to help Peter,' he said. 'Mrs Butts guessed why Peter ran away from the house. Going to the station was a long shot but I knew you had searched the town.'

Tina wanted to tell Peter about their scary ride but they couldn't talk about it in front of his dad.

Soon Peter's dad stood up. 'I have to get back to work,' he said, 'we have the talent competition tonight.'

'Dad works at the theatre,' said Peter. 'He organises the events.'

Mr Penrose said goodbye and left.

Peter looked so happy that Tina didn't really want to give him something to worry about. They had promised not to tell their secret but maybe Peter would know what to do.

As she began to speak she saw the look on Lesley's face. The more people who knew, the more dangerous it was for them and Lesley didn't trust Peter. Tina knew that, but now she had started she could not stop.

Caught!

That evening, the turning tide was pulling gently at the *Erica Banner*. Her mooring ropes were taut. The small white dinghy was floating behind her like a duckling behind its mother.

Tina and Peter hid behind some bushes in the small park near the marina. It was getting dark. There were only a few people about and no sign of the youths. Tina shivered and wished she'd brought a warmer jacket.

It had been Peter's idea to watch the yacht.

'Maybe they have called it off,' she said.

Peter shook his head. 'Not after all the planning. And why should they? They think they are safe.'

For once Tina wished she was in the theatre listening to Lesley sing. The truth was that she felt guilty not being there. She would be in trouble with her parents too.

'Wouldn't there be a crew to sail the yacht?' she whispered.

'Maybe one or two,' said Peter.

Something moved. Tina nudged Peter.

On one side of the yacht a small boat was moving in silently. Two figures rested the oars and stood up. They reached for the rope ladder hanging down the side of the yacht and began to climb.

It had begun!

Tina looked at Peter's face. He was

puzzled.

'Why the boat?' he said. 'They could just walk along the gangplank.'

He stood up. 'I'm going to see what's happening.'

'Don't be silly!' hissed Tina. 'Let's call for the police.' She reached into her pocket for her mobile.

But Peter was running across the gangplank and onto the deck of the yacht. Tina watched as he crept to one of the windows and peeped inside. Then he ran back to her.

'They're not going to steal the yacht. They are going to rob things from it! That's why they brought the small boat. I'm going to fix that.'

'What?'

'Put some water in their fuel tank. You stay here.'

He raced off again. As she watched he climbed down into the boat. If the thieves looked through the window now they would see him.

Time ticked by. Tina got fed up with waiting. She was not going to be left out.

She stood up and walked over to the yacht.

The door of the yacht's cabin was flung open. The two youths came out carrying bags. Peter had no time to get away; as he saw them he jumped into the water. But they had seen him, too. The taller one, Dave, dropped his bag and jumped straight into the water after him.

Bernie rushed over and grabbed Tina. 'You scream and the boyfriend doesn't come up for air,' he said. 'Get me?' He pushed Tina onto the yacht and into the cabin.

A moment later Dave pushed a dripping Peter inside. Tina looked at him, concerned. 'Are you OK?' she whispered.

'Where's your sister?' snapped Bernie.

'She's at the talent competition,' said Tina. Why had they been so stupid? They should have just called the police.

Dave nodded across to Bernie. 'OK, I'll tie them up while you get that cat.'

Tina looked at Peter. They weren't stealing the yacht or anything from it; they were taking Stuart Cresswell's Siamese cat. He would pay a lot to get it back.

Dave tied their hands and feet. Poor Peter was shivering with cold. They heard Bernie opening doors in the yacht.

Suddenly, there was a yowl and Bernie swore with pain. The cat was not coming quietly. Dave went to help and they came out with a struggling bundle.

Only the cat's cream oriental face could be seen and the blue eyes blazed with fury. The youths climbed down to the small boat.

'They won't get far,' said Peter through chattering teeth.

They heard the outboard motor start. Tina tried to huddle up to Peter to keep him warm.

'We have to phone the police,' said Peter. 'See if I can untie your hands.'

But his fingers were cold. Tina could feel them shaking.

He swore. 'I can't feel my fingers. Those lads will be back any minute.'

Tina knew the kidnappers would not be pleased when their boat stopped and their plans were ruined. They had planned it carefully and there was a lot of money at stake. Everyone knew how much Stuart Cresswell loved his cat. Everyone knew how rich he was too.

'Let me try,' said Tina. She felt for the knots around his wrist but water had soaked into it. She winced as one of her fingernails broke.

Then they both heard the sound of footsteps thud onto the deck and the cabin door was wrenched open.

Reward

Two policemen came in. Stuart Cresswell was with them.

'Peppa, have they taken Peppa?' he said.

'Yes,' said Peter, 'they took the cat. We thought they were going to steal the yacht and tried to stop them. They won't have got far though because I put water in the fuel tank.'

The singer's face relaxed. 'I just hope they haven't hurt my poor cat.'

Tina's parents came to the door.

'What's happening? Where's Lesley?' said her dad. 'She disappeared and did not come on stage for the prizes, we thought she'd be with you.'

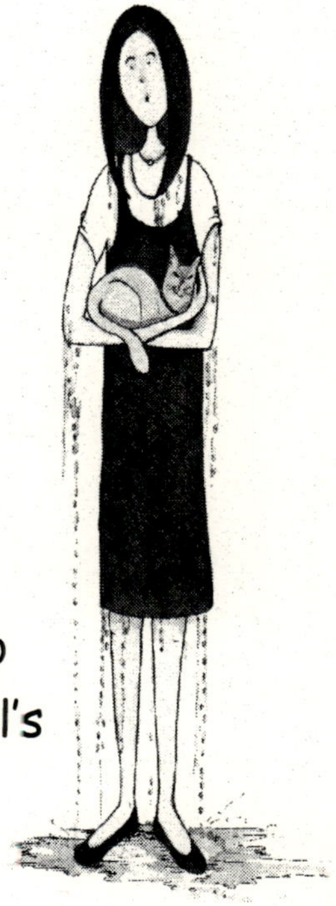

Then Lesley arrived, dripping and shivering. She was holding the cat. Tina watched as she came into the cabin and put the cat into Stuart's arms. Lesley, who was afraid of the water, had jumped in to save a cat! Stuart Cresswell's cat.

Stuart took the cat. He went into the bathroom and came out with some towels. He handed one to Lesley and one to Peter. Then he began to dry Peppa with another. Her loud purr made everyone laugh.

The police had taken one look inside the cabin and then had gone to catch the youths.

Tina turned to Lesley. 'How did you end up in the water anyway? You were supposed to be at the theatre!'

'Well, I noticed you were not in the audience and I guessed you'd be checking on the *Erica Banner.* I thought I'd join you. On my way, I heard the cat fighting her way out of the bag and she managed to jump out of the boat, onto a rock surrounded by water, so I went to get her . . .'

'How did the police know?' asked Peter.

'I asked someone to call before I jumped in to save the cat,' said Lesley.

Another person came to the door. It was Peter's father. Tina watched as he smiled at his son and came to put an arm round his shoulders.

'What's happening here?' he asked. 'Are you all right, Mr Cresswell?'

Stuart smiled. 'These brave young people stopped my cat from being *cat*napped,' he said. 'I never imagined anyone would steal her and make me pay to get her back.'

He looked round and smiled. 'Thank you all very much. How would you like to sail over to Jersey with me tomorrow? I'm doing a concert there and you three are invited.'

Lesley's eyes glowed. 'We'd love to,' she said.

'And you didn't collect your prize, did you? You came second in the competition.'

Everyone clapped and Lesley grinned.

Tina went over to Peter.

'I'm staying for the rest of the holidays,' he said. 'Maybe for good. Dad is going to talk to Mum.'

'Great!' she said. She was pleased for him and it also meant that they could spend a bit more time together.

He thrust his hand into his pocket. 'By the way, here's the money I owe you.'

Tina smiled. She'd been right about him all along.

Also available from

e PRINT

PUBLISHING

The One that Got Away by Stephanie Baudet
ISBN 978-1-900818-87-2

When Mike and Sophie have the idea of looking after small pets while their owners are on holiday, they think it will be an easy way of making some pocket money. But some of the pets are not quite what they had bargained for. And when one of them escapes, there's no telling where it will end up...

The Curse of the Full Moon by Stephanie Baudet
ISBN 978-1-904904-11-3

One afternoon Simon is frightened by a ghostly figure in the woods. Later on he learns about the legend of the Green Man, a spirit protecting the woods, said to put a curse on anyone cutting trees. The council has decided to build new houses and a sports centre in place of the woods. Simon is devasted to learn that his best friend's dad is the builder contracted for the job...

A Marrow Escape by Stephanie Baudet
ISBN 978-1-900818-82-7

Dad has flu and it's Kelly's job to look after his prize marrow. But when it goes missing she needs to work hard to stop him from finding out. Can she get the prize veggie back in time for the big competition on Saturday? With the help of her brother Zac and his friends, the chase is on...

The Owlers by Stephanie Baudet
ISBN 978-1-904904-87-8

Jack's father is a fisherman involved in smuggling. Due to stormy weather, the boats have been hauled onto the beach. When the Prime Minister learns this, he orders soldiers to come and burn the boats in order to put a stop to smuggling. Jack goes in search of his father who is missing, and becomes caught up in a battle as the townsfolk try to prevent the soldiers from burning the boats.

The Mum Manager by Suzi Cresswell
ISBN 978-1-905637-45-4

Toby plays for a successful football team. But there's a problem; the manager is leaving the area and Toby's mum, Sharon, a hairdresser and yoga teacher, is the only volunteer to take on the role. Will she be up to the challenge? Toby doubts it as the first training session involves yoga, dance routines and lots of chatting...

Jade Fry, Private Eye by Suzi Cresswell
ISBN 978-1-905637-75-1

Jade is fed up when she has to stay with her Gran. But life there is more exciting than expected as she is soon swept up in an exciting adventure involving Gran's pony, Captain. Captain is important to Gran's friend, a race horse trainer whose star horse, Smithy, is due to run in the Melton Chase soon. Without Captain by his side Smithy won't get into the horse box. But it seems that someone wants to stop him competing when Captain disappears. Jade turns detective and follows the trail to find out what is going on...

Porky Pies by Suzi Cresswell
ISBN 978-1-905637-66-9

Jaz has a bad habit - he can't stop telling little white lies. When he joins a new school, he tells his classmates that he's the son of pop star Rocky Riff. Jaz finds himself in big trouble when Aisha turns out to be his greatest fan and Clint demands proof...

Close Call by Sandra Glover
ISBN 978-1-905637-07-2

MP's daughter, Anna, is worried when she overhears a telephone conversation between her dad and a mystery caller. She's even more concerned when her dad lies about the call. What might her dad be mixed up in? And does it have anything to do with the strange young man who's been watching the house?

Cracking Up by Sandra Glover
ISBN 978-1-904904-86-1
Selected for the SLA Boys into Books (5-11) 2008 List.

With his mum in hospital and stressed at school thanks to his awful teacher, Jamie thinks his life can't possibly get any worse. Until he meets a lollipop lady who thinks she is a fairy godmother. It's all nonsense - but why do wishes suddenly start coming true, with disastrous consequences?

Beastly Things in the Barn by Sandra Glover
ISBN 978-1-904904-96-0

Farmer's son Mark is delighted when they manage to rent their newly converted barn to a family for the summer. But Mark's delight turns to horror when the Beesley-Trings, quickly renamed the Beastly Things, arrive. They are completely mad and even worse, they seem determined to ruin Mark's life. Still, it's only for six weeks, so it can't be that bad...or can it?

The Bears Bite Back by Derek Keilty
ISBN 978-1-905637-36-2

This is a humorous and wacky sequel to *Goldilocks and the Three Bears.* The three bears are fuming after the ringleted prowler has left their place in disarray. They quickly decide to get their own back by following the intruder's footprints and marching over to her house to eat her food, break her furniture and sleep in her bed!

Magic Beans on Toast by Derek Keilty
ISBN 978-1-905637-58-4

Zoe plants a magic bean and is soon scaling an enormous beanstalk to Giant Land where she is captured by the grandsons of the Giant from *Jack and the Beanstalk*..

The Mummy's Finger by Ian MacDonald
ISBN 978-1-905637-77-5

When on a trip to the museum a mummified finger mysteriously slips from a glass case and falls in Owen's pocket, it spells big trouble! Owen and Chaz are investigating, and the ancient mummy's curse is invoked. The boys battle against a plague of scorpions, the stinging arrows of resurrected warriors... even the mummy's missus is on the trail in this hilarious chase to return the mummy's finger!

The Haunted Windmill by Margaret Nash
ISBN 978-1-904904-22-9

Jade feels uneasy as she stands with her school class inside the local windmill. Kate Slingsby, the lady who owns the windmill, is telling the children about its history. When someone asks if the windmill has a ghost, Kate Slingsby mysteriously replies, 'Don't all old places have a ghost?'